kirigami

the art of cutting & folding paper

Ho Huu An
Laurence Arnac

contents

the origins of kirigami

The word kirigami is actually a modern Japanese term that takes its influence from the art of paper folding known as origami. Today, kirigami is widely associated with paper cutting, folding and handmade pop-up cards. The etymology of the word comes from the Japanese '*kiru*': to cut, and '*gami*': paper.

Both kirigami and origami have their roots in '*jian zhi*', the original Chinese papercutting art that dates back to the fourth and fifth centuries A.D. – two centuries after the invention of paper in China. In Japan, '*jian zhi*' appeared in the seventh century and gave rise to origami and, subsequently, kirigami (as well as a variety of other techniques). Kirigami is still used today in the Shinto religion for special ceremonies.

Originally, '*jian zhi*' was mainly practised in monasteries due to the high cost of paper, and the subjects of its art were all religious. Nowadays, '*jian zhi*' can encompass a variety of different papercutting techniques and is used to decorate the home during such events as the Chinese Lunar New Year or Spring Festival.

Over the centuries, this Oriental art form has spread throughout the world. There is even evidence of it in Europe dating back to the seventeenth century. Throughout various cultures it has inspired many new and different techniques, including:
- '*spitzenbild*' or lace pictures cut from paper and mainly practised by nuns in Switzerland, Germany, Austria, the Netherlands and France who considered papercutting to be a meditative or contemplative technique
- the art of the silhouette in France and Switzerland with '*tableaux en découpures*' (large prints cut in vellum) popularised by Jean Huber in the eighteenth century
- shadow portraits, popular in the nineteenth century
- '*wycinanki*', a traditional and popular Polish folk craft comprising paper cutouts in bright colours. Used to decorate homes during the main religious festivals and family celebrations
- '*ketubah*', traditional Jewish prenuptial agreements cut by artists and combining cutouts, calligraphy and painting.

There are many contemporary artists, painters and visual artists who have used, and still use, the techniques of papercutting in their works including Matisse, Kara Walker, and many more.

materials

To achieve the best results, it is recommended that you obtain the following basic materials:

• a hobby knife (a tool with detachable blades attached to a handle with a precision blade for intricate detail)
• a special cutting mat
(self-healing mat in A4 or A3 format)
• a metal craft ruler
• a paper folder
• adhesive
• paper (between 140gsm/52lbs and 180gsm/67lbs)

Cutting out

The hobby knife will enable you to make the kind of cuts that may sometimes be as fine as lace. You will need this tool for instances where other blades are too unwieldy and could tear the paper.

Remember that this tool should be used with caution, as it is extremely sharp. Always take care and work slowly. When cutting, avoid placing the hand that is holding the paper in the trajectory of the cutting blade. Change the blade regularly for optimum cutting.

The cutting mat is an indispensable tool for making your kirigami. Being pliable, it prevents the paper from slipping and enables the blade to trace the cut without wavering.

Folding

The paper folder is an indispensable tool. It is often made from bone and is designed to help you mark your creases, which are integral for accurate folding and assembly. The line creases are indicated in the diagrams as either: mountain folds (dash-dot lines) or valley folds (dash lines).

Paper

You can obtain a wide range of paper in different colours and finishes (avoid paper that is too fibrous or uneven as more difficult to cut). The same applies to its thickness, which is expressed in grams per square metre (gsm) or pounds (lbs).

An ideal weight to start out with is 160gsm (59lbs) paper, which is a good compromise, being neither too fine nor too rigid (a more economical option is to purchase reams of A4 paper from larger stores or craft shops).

how to cut

Take some time to familiarise yourself with the hobby knife, learning how to manipulate it carefully with your hand. By mastering confident, precise movements, you will achieve the desired result. For each project, photocopy or scan in the pages, then print your desired patterns on to A4 paper (refer to the section on materials); it is possible to enlarge the patterns by adjusting the scale by up to 120% using the options on your printer. You need to work on the reverse side of the sheet so that the printed lines are not visible when the pattern is finally assembled.

The basics of cutting out

Use the worksheet on page 8 and start by cutting a series of straight lines, then continue with other shapes (zigzags, curves, geometric shapes, etc.). By practising in advance, you will get used to the action of the blade on the paper, so that you can adjust your movement to the outline of the subject.

By keeping your hand relaxed, you will intuitively find the right balance between firmness and fluidity. Eventually you will find a position where you feel completely at ease making your cuts. Always avoid holding the hobby knife in a vertical position as the blade will not glide and will tear the paper.

By remaining relaxed, your wrist exerts pressure on the blade of the hobby knife due to the slight inclination in which it is held (around 45°).

With your other hand, hold the sheet of paper flat. Make sure that your hand is not in the trajectory of the cut. When cutting curves or circles, the hand that holds the paper always pivots the paper following the trajectory of the cut, a bit like using a sewing machine where the needle stays still and the fabric is guided in the direction of the seam.

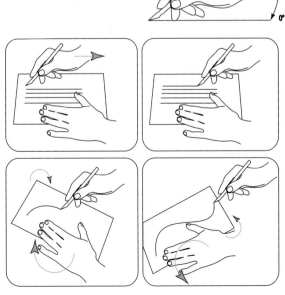

practice cuts

cutting out and assembly

Under each of the project titles the level of difficulty for both folding and cutting is indicated by the following icon: ⬦
Use the icons to determine the level of difficulty ranging from ⬦ (easy) to ⬦⬦⬦ (difficult).

On each pattern template:
- continuous lines indicate cutting lines
- dash lines indicate that the crease is at the bottom (valley fold) and dash-dot lines indicate that the crease is at the top (mountain fold)

————— cut

- - - - - - valley fold

- · - · - · mountain fold

Assembly techniques are in two forms: cards opening at 90° or at 180°.

For a 90° assembly, certain proportions must be adhered to once the card has been folded. In the example below for a simple, one level card, if the design to be attached measures 10mm (½in) in depth, then the distance between the centre fold and the bottom fold of the design (base) must be the same (i.e. 10mm [½in] here).

90° card

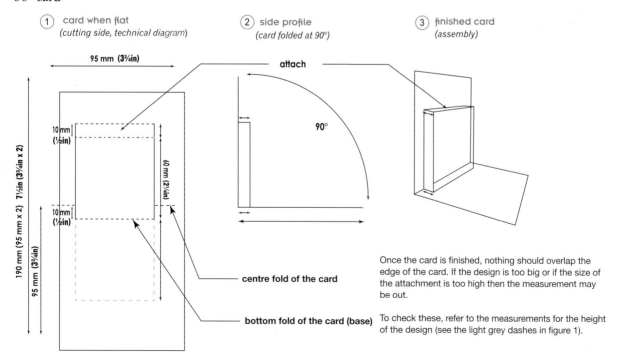

① card when flat
(cutting side, technical diagram)

② side profile
(card folded at 90°)

③ finished card
(assembly)

95 mm (3¾in)

attach

90°

10 mm (½in)

60 mm (2⅜in)

10 mm (½in)

190 mm (95 mm x 2)   7½in (3¾in x 2)

95 mm (3¾in)

centre fold of the card

bottom fold of the card (base)

Once the card is finished, nothing should overlap the edge of the card. If the design is too big or if the size of the attachment is too high then the measurement may be out.

To check these, refer to the measurements for the height of the design (see the light grey dashes in figure 1).

cutting out and assembly (cont'd)

180° cards

This flat angle, as it is known in geometry, opens up some interesting options for creativity.

In this model, the kirigami is created on two parts that complement one another, as in the example below.

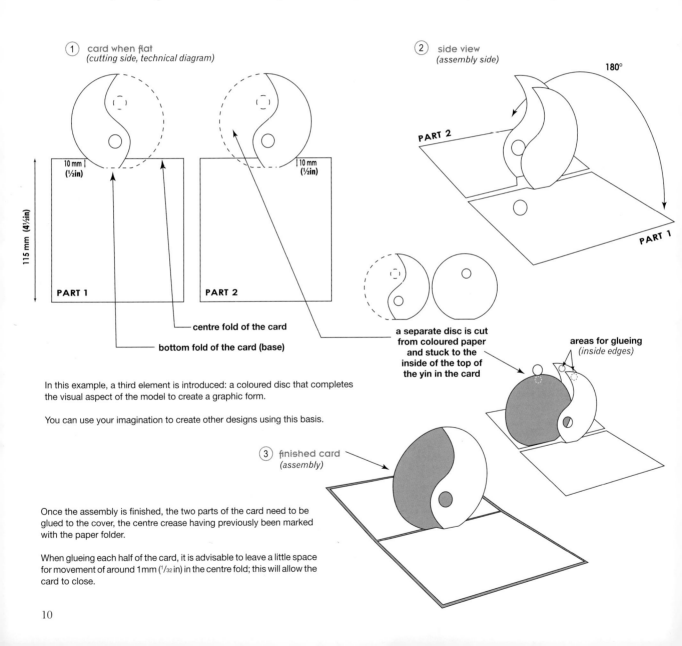

① card when flat
(cutting side, technical diagram)

115 mm (4½in)

10 mm (½in)

10 mm (½in)

PART 1

PART 2

centre fold of the card

bottom fold of the card (base)

② side view
(assembly side)

180°

PART 2

PART 1

a separate disc is cut from coloured paper and stuck to the inside of the top of the yin in the card

areas for glueing
(inside edges)

③ finished card
(assembly)

In this example, a third element is introduced: a coloured disc that completes the visual aspect of the model to create a graphic form.

You can use your imagination to create other designs using this basis.

Once the assembly is finished, the two parts of the card need to be glued to the cover, the centre crease having previously been marked with the paper folder.

When glueing each half of the card, it is advisable to leave a little space for movement of around 1 mm (¹/₃₂ in) in the centre fold; this will allow the card to close.

basic templates for card covers:

90° card template

Assembly of a 90° card

actual size

enlarge to 125 %

rectangular cover – plain

cutting
folding

square cover - plain

cutting
folding

actual size

square cover – flowers

cutting
folding

actual size

poppies

cutting ♦♦♦
folding ♦

side 1

180° card

Laurence Arnac

actual size

side 2

180° card

Laurence Arnac

actual size

bulldog

cutting
folding

180° card

Laurence Arnac

actual size

side 2

180° card

Laurence Arnac

actual size

butterfly

cutting ♦♦♦
folding ♦

side 1

180° card

Once the two halves of the card have been cut out, glue them inside a cover and then apply a little spot of adhesive in the centre of the spiral (part B) that you now pull out and glue to the mark (the little dot) on part A.

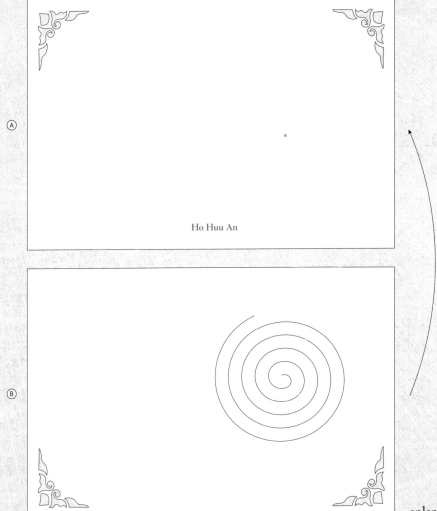

Ho Huu An

enlarge to 143 %

side 2

180° card

To assemble the wings of the butterfly, link the two notches together (male and female), then fold them slightly.

Having assembled the butterfly, glue it along the centre to the spiral on the card (side 1), as shown in the photograph.

notch f
(female)

notch m
(male)

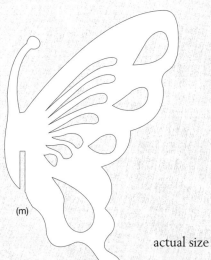

(f)

(m)

actual size

celestial sphere

cutting ♦♦♦
folding ♦♦♦

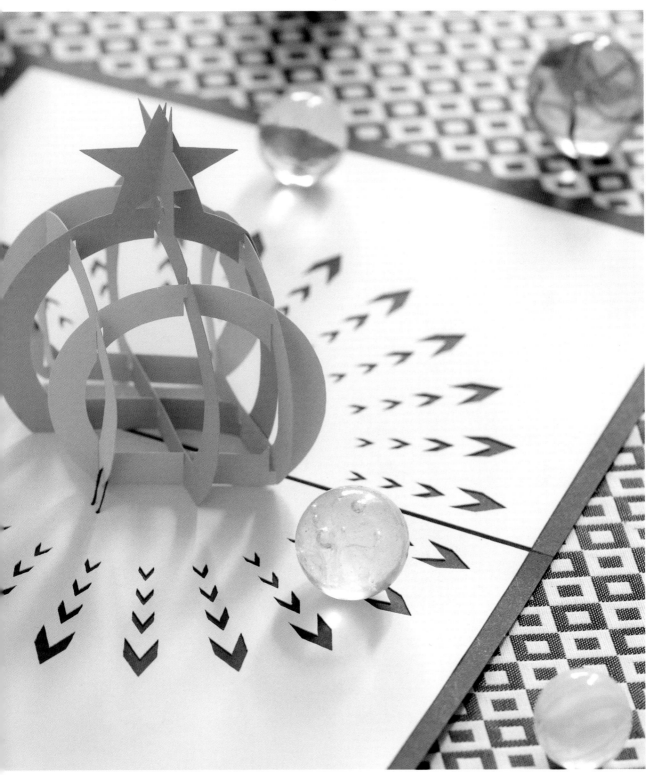

side 1

180° card

The six pieces to be cut out below will form a sphere. To assemble, link each female notch with its corresponding male notch following the numbers.

The two small holes at the bottom of parts C and D are for the thread which will attach the sphere via two corresponding holes in the base card (side 2).

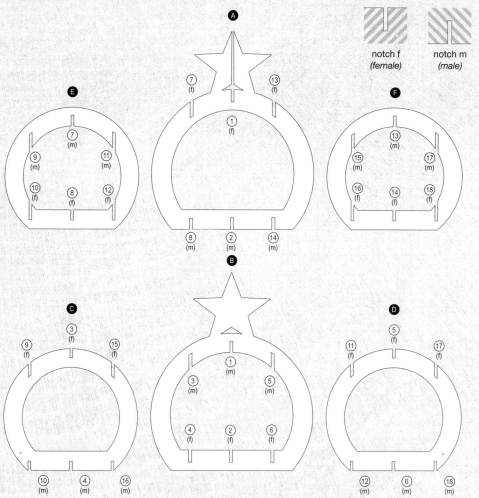

enlarge to 125 %

side 2

180° card

Once the sphere has been sewn into both halves of the card, glue the card on to a cover that has already been folded in half (the knots of the sewing threads located underneath the card will then be invisible).

Ho Huu An

enlarge to 125%

Bounce Bounce!

Ho Huu An

kangaroo

cutting 🌢🌢
folding 🌢🌢

actual size

palm tree

cutting ♦♦♦
folding ♦

side 1

180° card

Once the card has been cut
out and stuck to the inside of
a cover, join the pop-up sides
by fitting the notches of each
palm tree into one another.

actual size

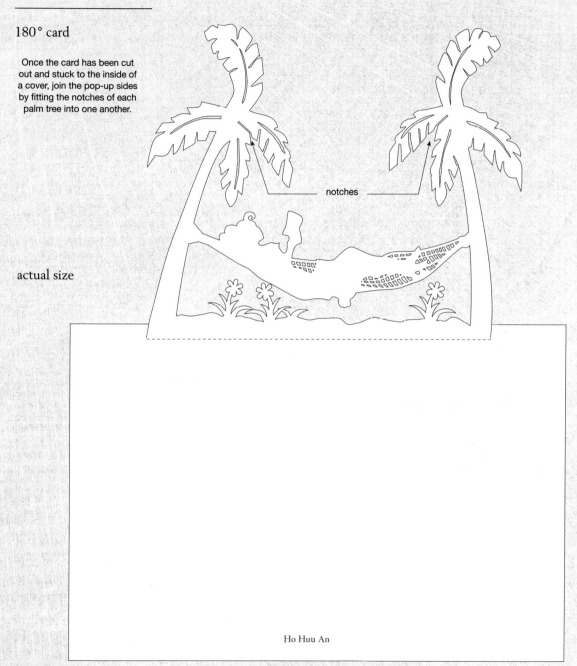

notches

Ho Huu An

side 2

180° card

notches

actual size

Ho Huu An

gift box

cutting ▲▲▲
folding ▲▲▲

side 1

180° card

The six pieces for cutting out below will form a gift box.
To assemble, link each (female) notch with its corresponding (male) notch following the numbered sequence.
The two small holes at the bottom of pieces E and F are for the thread to pass through when sewing the gift box into the base card (side 2).

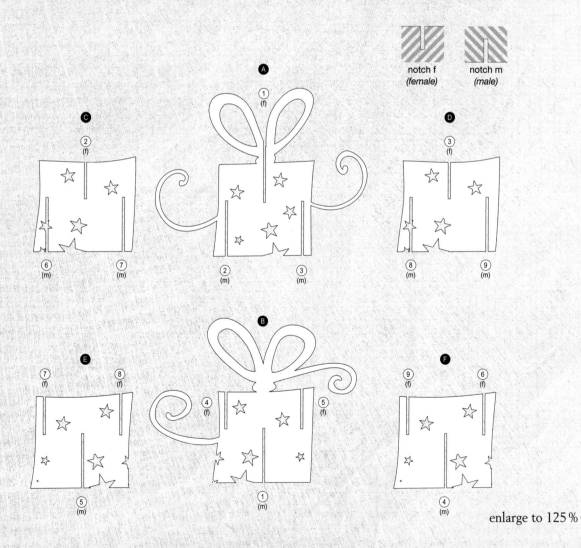

enlarge to 125%

side 2

180° card

Once the gift box has been sewn into each half of the card, glue the card into a cover that has already been folded in half (the knots of the sewing threads located underneath the card will then be invisible).

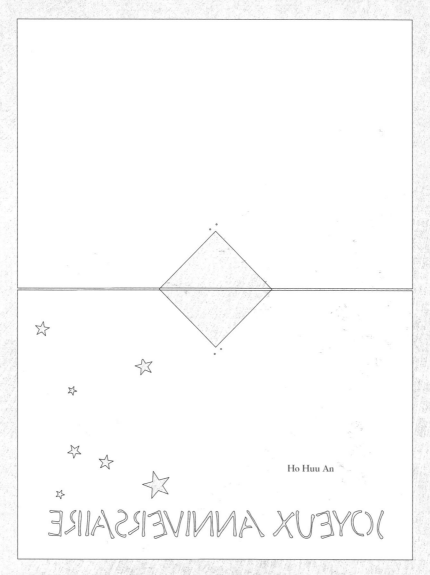

Ho Huu An

enlarge to 125 %

Ho Huu An

piano

cutting ♦♦
folding ♦♦

actual size

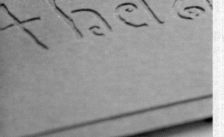

cats

cutting
folding

side 1

180° card

Print and cut out the cat motifs above using paper that is a different colour to the card, then glue them to the corresponding areas of the sides of the pop-up card.

Happy Birthday

Ho Huu An

enlarge to 133%

side 2

180° card

Ho Huu An

enlarge to 133%

Ho Huu An

enlarge to 125%

owl

cutting
folding

dragonfly

cutting ●●
folding ●

side 1

180° card

Laurence Arnac

actual size

side 2

180° card

Laurence Arnac

actual size

cat with hearts

cutting   ♦♦
folding   ♦

180° card

Laurence Arnac

actual size

side 2

180° card

Laurence Arnac

actual size

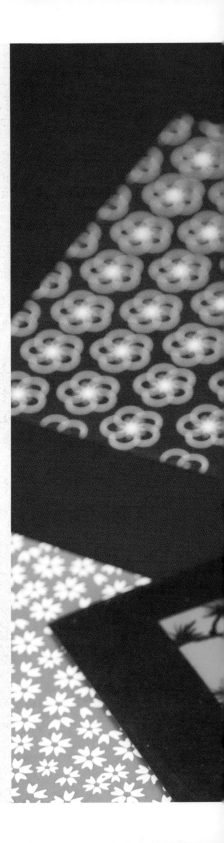

bonsai

cutting
folding

side 1

Cut the pattern below into the front of the cover.

Ho Huu An

enlarge to 125 %

side 2

Glue a plain inner card to the inside of the cover.

enlarge to 125%

fairy

cutting 💧💧
folding 💧

side 1

180° card

Laurence Arnac

actual size

side 2

180° card

Laurence Arnac

actual size

toadstools

cutting ●●●
folding ●●

side 1

180° card

Print and cut out the motifs below and opposite using
paper in different colours from the card.
Glue them to the corresponding areas on both sides
of the pop-up card.

Ho Huu An

enlarge to 133 %

side 2

180° card

Ho Huu An

enlarge to 133%

swallows

cutting   ♦♦♦
folding   ♦

180° card

Laurence Arnac

actual size

side 2

180° card

Laurence Arnac

actual size

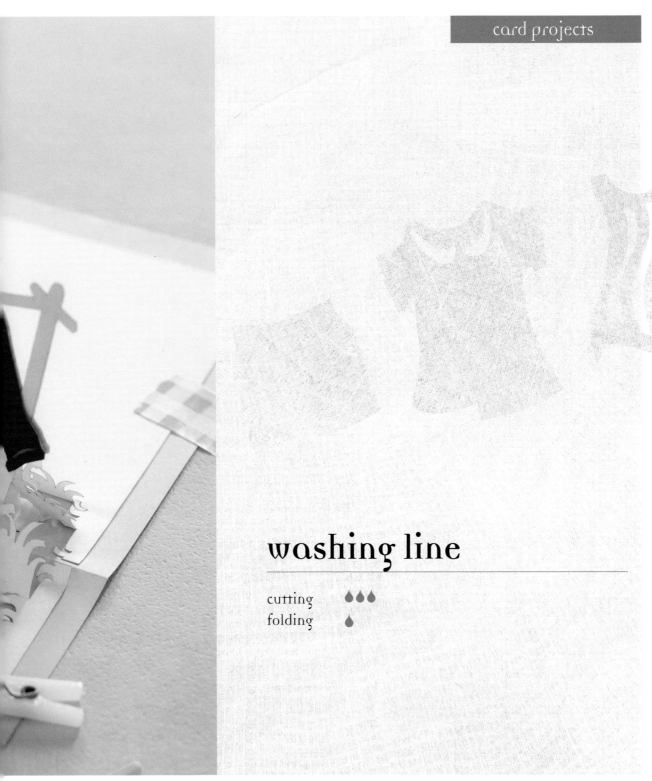

washing line

cutting ♦♦♦
folding ♦

side 1

180° card

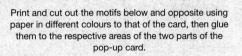

Print and cut out the motifs below and opposite using paper in different colours to that of the card, then glue them to the respective areas of the two parts of the pop-up card.

Ho Huu An

enlarge to 133%

76

side 2

180° card

Ho Huu An

enlarge to 133 %

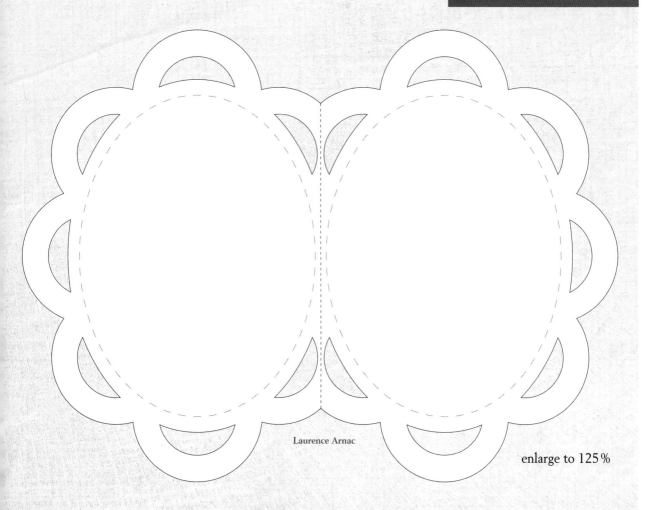

Laurence Arnac

enlarge to 125 %

fish platter

cutting
folding

180° card for the outside cover.
Cut out and fold in half.

side 1

180° - inside card

After cutting out all the patterns, follow the diagram (below, top right) and glue the two sides of the inner card (the ovals containing the fish bone motif) on to the cover card. Insert the text cards into the slots on the pop-up cards, then glue these two pop-up halves to each other to complete the card.

When finished, this double-sided menu is left open at 180° (see photo).

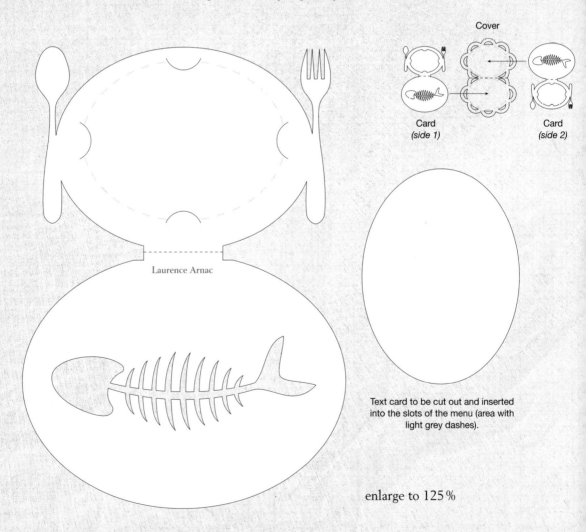

Laurence Arnac

Cover

Card
(side 1)

Card
(side 2)

Text card to be cut out and inserted into the slots of the menu (area with light grey dashes).

enlarge to 125 %

side 2

180° - inside card

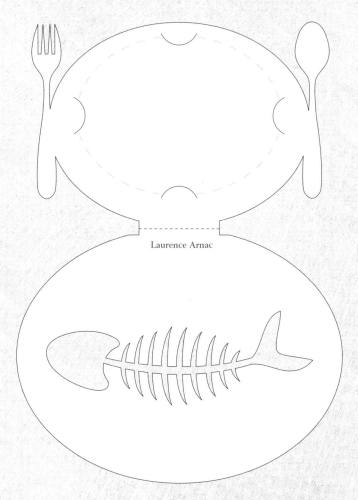

Laurence Arnac

Text card to be cut out and inserted
into the slots of the platter (area with
light grey dashes).

enlarge to 125 %

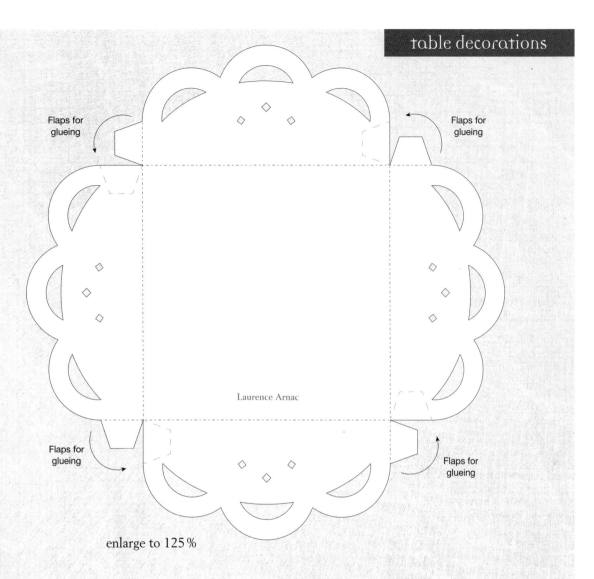

Flaps for glueing

Flaps for glueing

Flaps for glueing

Flaps for glueing

Laurence Arnac

enlarge to 125 %

blue basket

cutting
folding

After cutting out and folding the pattern, assemble the basket by glueing the flaps on to their respective edges (indicated by the light grey dashes).

zigzag menu

cutting
folding

actual size

Laurence Arnac

MENU

side 2

The text cards below are to be cut out and inserted into the slots in the zigzag menu.

actual size

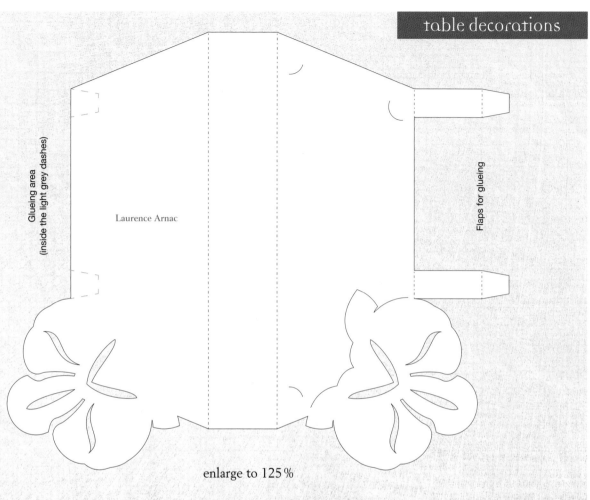

Glueing area
(inside the light grey dashes)

Laurence Arnac

Flaps for glueing

enlarge to 125%

orchid
place-name holders

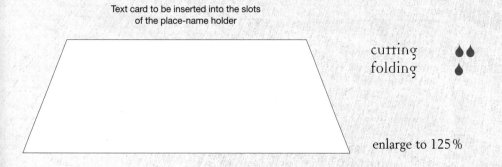

Text card to be inserted into the slots
of the place-name holder

cutting
folding

enlarge to 125%

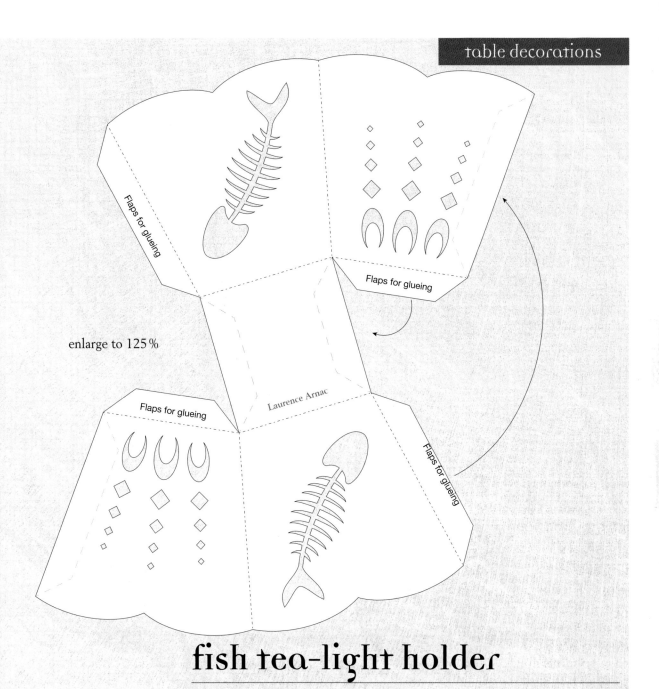

enlarge to 125 %

Flaps for glueing

Flaps for glueing

Flaps for glueing

Flaps for glueing

Laurence Arnac

fish tea-light holder

cutting   🌢🌢
folding   🌢

After cutting out and folding the pattern, assemble the tea-light holder by glueing the flaps on to their respective areas (indicated by light grey dashes).

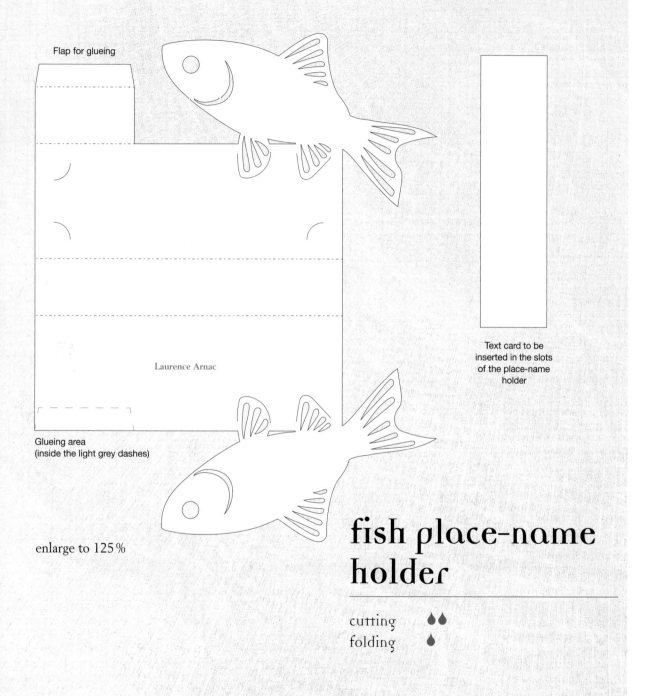

Flap for glueing

Glueing area
(inside the light grey dashes)

Laurence Arnac

Text card to be
inserted in the slots
of the place-name
holder

enlarge to 125%

fish place-name holder

cutting

folding

orchid invitations

cutting
folding

side 1

'Orchid' invitation with
two flaps.

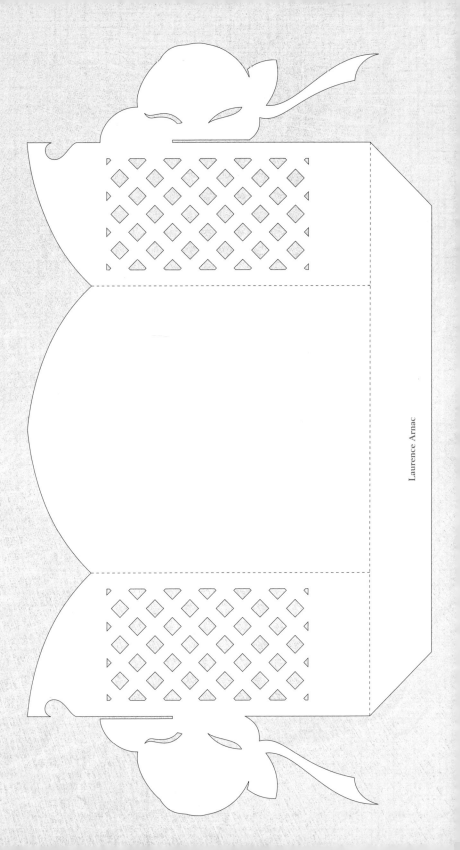

Laurence Arnac

actual size

side 2

The text cards below are to be cut out and slipped inside the 'Orchid' invitation with two flaps.

actual size

Laurence Arnac

Flaps for glueing

Flaps for glueing

Flaps for glueing

Flaps for glueing

little orchid basket

enlarge to 125 %

cutting ♦♦

folding ♦

After cutting out and folding the pattern, assemble the basket by glueing the flaps on to their respective areas (indicated by light grey dashes).

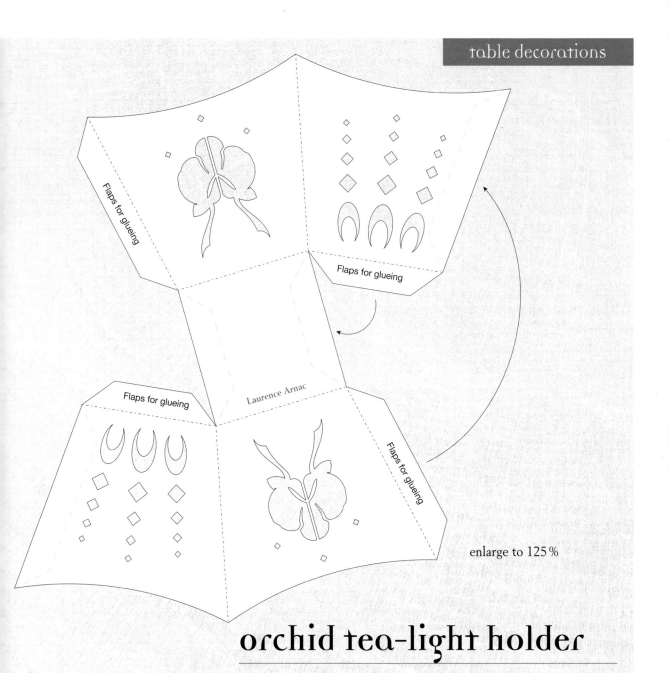

Laurence Arnac

enlarge to 125 %

orchid tea-light holder

cutting 🌢🌢
folding 🌢

After cutting out and folding the pattern, assemble the tea-light holder by glueing the flaps on to their respective areas (indicated by the light grey dashes).

Laurence Arnac

enlarge to 125 %

decorative bauble

cutting 🌢🌢
assembly 🌢🌢

Photocopy this pattern eight times. Cut out sixteen sections to be fixed at the top and bottom by inserting each of the slots into the corresponding slots of each disc. (Two discs for sixteen branches = one decoration.)

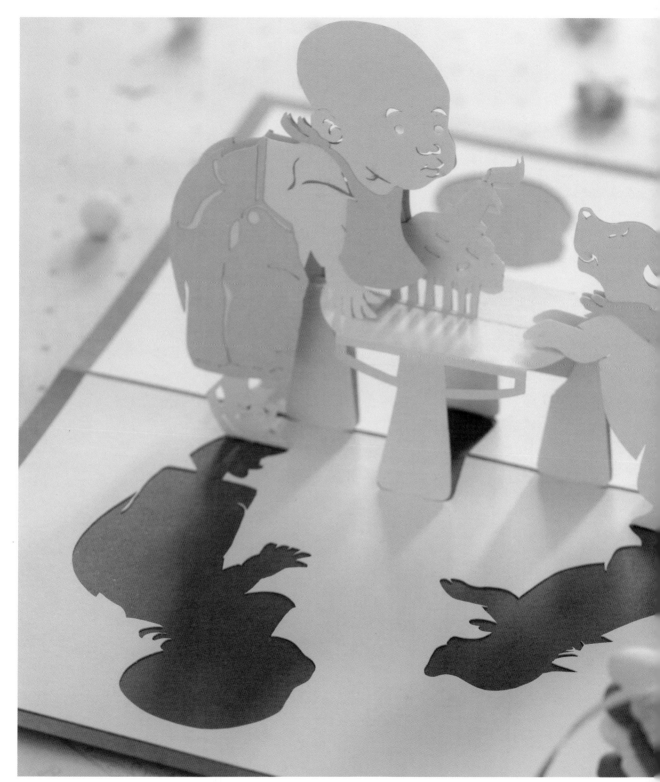

baby card

cutting ♦♦♦
folding ♦♦

side 1

180° card

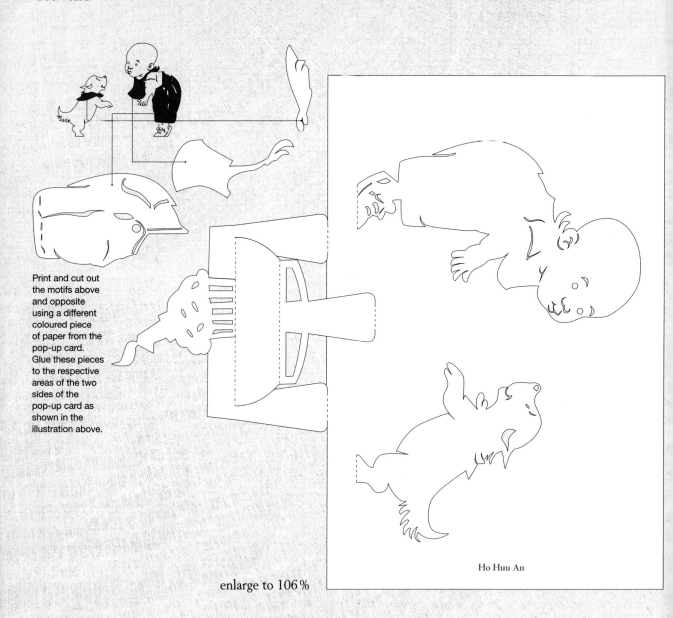

Print and cut out the motifs above and opposite using a different coloured piece of paper from the pop-up card. Glue these pieces to the respective areas of the two sides of the pop-up card as shown in the illustration above.

Ho Huu An

enlarge to 106%

side 2

180° card

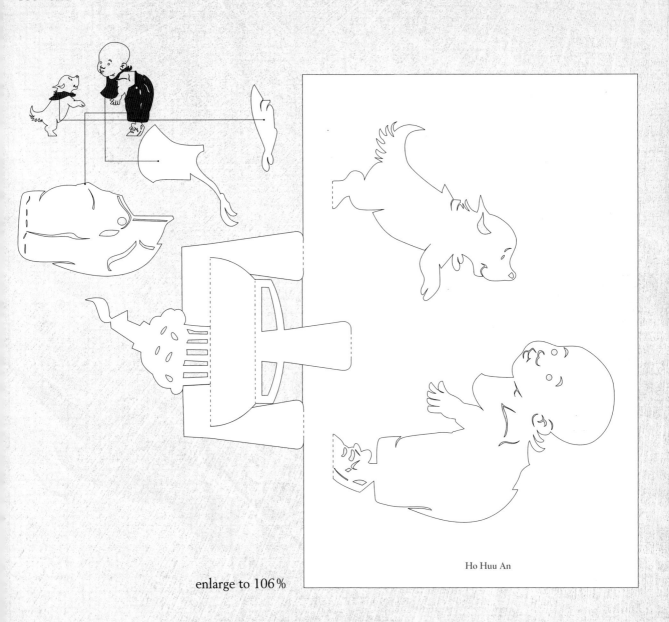

Ho Huu An

enlarge to 106%

wedding

cutting
folding

180° card

Ho Huu An

actual size

side 2

180° card

Ho Huu An

actual size

thank-you card

cutting ◆◆◆
folding ◆◆

180° card

Merci

Print and cut out the '*Merci*' motif above using a piece of paper in a different colour from the pop-up card. Glue them to the heart shapes on the pop-up card.

Once the card has been assembled and glued inside on to cover, join the butterfly together using 'male' and 'female' notches (see page 27).

actual size

Ho Huu An

side 2

180° card

Merci

Once the card has been assembled and glued inside the cover, join the butterfly together using 'male' and 'female' notches (see page 27).

actual size

Ho Huu An

90° card

Print and cut out the hearts below using a piece of paper in a different colour from the pop-up card. Then glue them on top of the hearts on the pop-up card.

Laurence Arnac

love

cutting 🌢🌢🌢
folding 🌢🌢

actual size

congratulations

cutting
folding

side 1

180° card

Print and cut out the motifs right and opposite using a piece of paper in a different colour from the card. Glue them to the respective areas on each of the two pop-up card sides.

Ho Huu An

enlarge to 105%

side 2

180° card

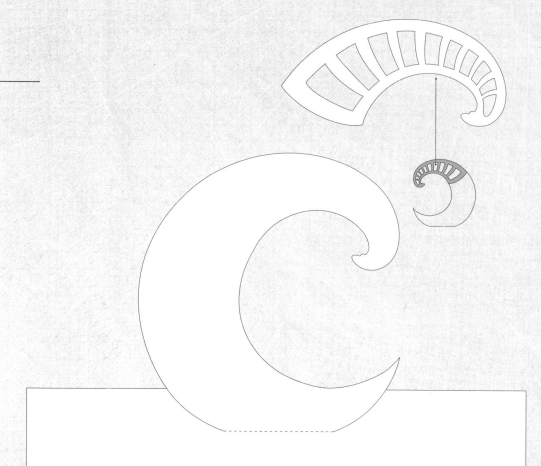

Ho Huu An

enlarge to 105%

Laurence Arnac

enlarge to 133 %

christmas wall decoration

cutting ♦♦♦

Flap for glueing

actual size

Laurence Arnac

reindeer

cutting 🌢🌢
folding 🌢

Area for glueing

Laurence Arnac

actual size

hanging angel

cutting 🌢🌢

Laurence Arnac

enlarge to 133 %

hanging snowflake

cutting ◆◆◆

Laurence Arnac

actual size

christmas bauble

cutting ◆◆◆
assembly ◆◆

Photocopy the pattern above eight times. Cut out sixteen sections to be fixed at the top and bottom by inserting the slots into the corresponding slots of each disc. (Two discs for sixteen branches = one bauble.) Photocopy and cut out the templates for the top and bottom of the bauble. Assemble as on page 103. Thread string through the holes in the top to hang the bauble.

nativity card

cutting
folding

side 1

180° card

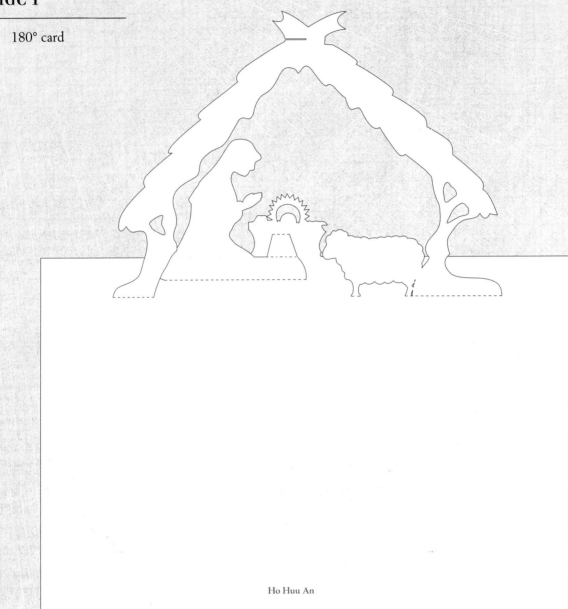

Ho Huu An

actual size

side 2

180° card

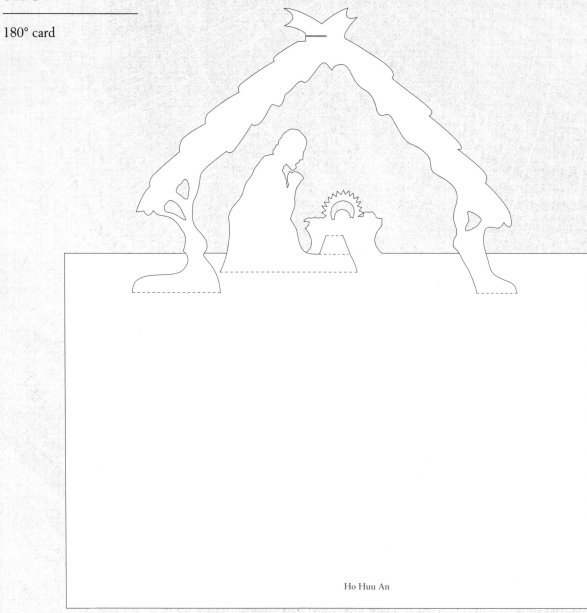

Ho Huu An

actual size

Slot
Ⓑ

Laurence Arnac

Ⓐ
Slot

actual size

hanging star

cutting 🌢🌢
assembly 🌢

Once the two stars have been cut out, slide
slot A into slot B to assemble (see photo).

christmas tree

cutting
folding

side 1

180° card

Print and cut out the templates, and attach them inside the cover. Glue the two sides of the tree together. Glue the top of the line of stars from side 1 to the top of the stars from side 2 to form an arch, as shown in the photograph on page 139.

Ho Huu An

actual size

side 2

180° card

Ho Huu An

actual size

Flaps for glueing

Flaps for glueing

enlarge to 133 %

Laurence Arnac

Flaps for glueing

Flaps for glueing

snowflake tea-light holder

cutting

folding

After cutting out and folding the pattern, assemble the tea-light holder by glueing the flaps on to their respective areas (indicated by light grey dashes).

angel card

cutting
folding

side 1

180° card

JOYEUX

Ho Huu An

side 2

180° card

Ho Huu An

actual size

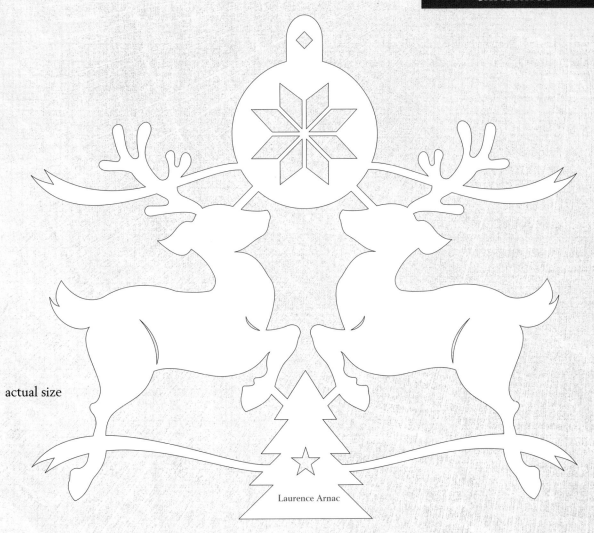

actual size

Laurence Arnac

reindeer wall-hanging

cutting ♦♦

snowflake wall-hanging

cutting ♦♦♦

Laurence Arnac

actual size

snowflake garland

cutting

side 1

Photocopy then cut out the snowflakes for the garland, making as many copies as you need for the desired length (the snowflakes are joined together by threading through the holes at each end).

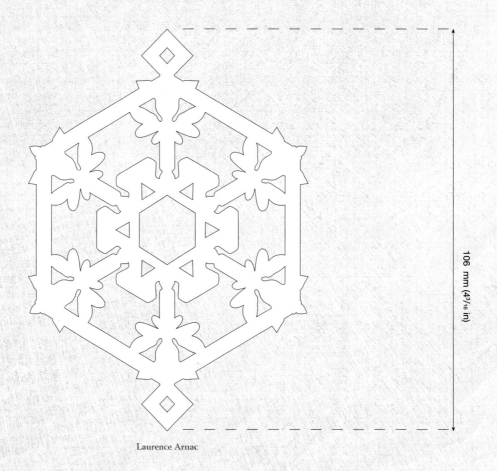

Laurence Arnac

106 mm (4⁹/₁₆ in)

actual size

side 2

140 mm (5½ in)

actual size

Laurence Arnac

Laurence Arnac

snowflake card

cutting ♦♦
folding ♦

actual size

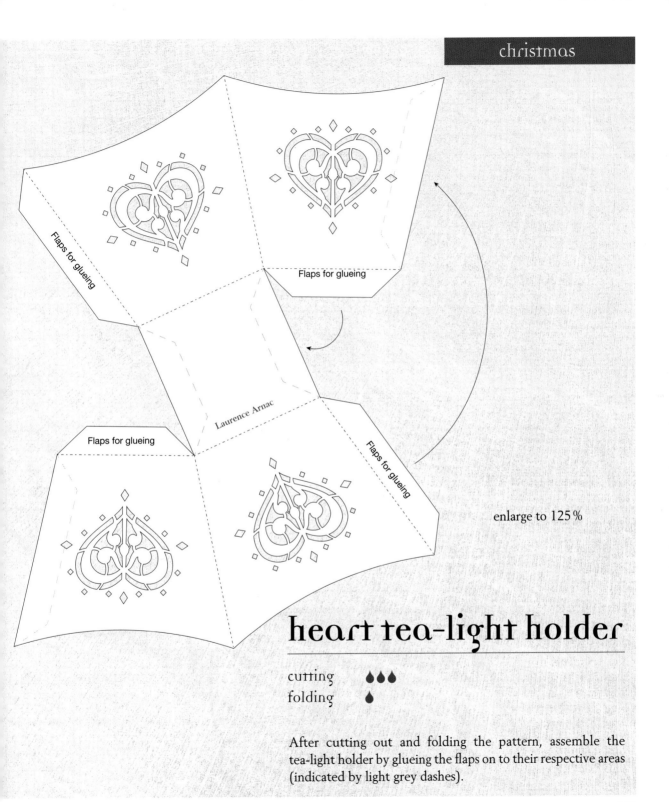

Flaps for glueing

Flaps for glueing

Flaps for glueing

Flaps for glueing

Laurence Arnac

enlarge to 125 %

heart tea-light holder

cutting   ◆◆◆
folding   ◆

After cutting out and folding the pattern, assemble the
tea-light holder by glueing the flaps on to their respective areas
(indicated by light grey dashes).

159

acknowledgements

Images from:

Petit Pan (www.petitpan.com): paper p. 21, background fabric p. 98
La Droguerie (www.ladroguerie.com): flower p. 32
Hema (www.hema.fr): plate and fabric p. 78
Lama Li (www.lamali.com): paper p. 85
Gien (www.gien.com): plates p. 100
Fleux (www.fleux.com): rabbit p. 142

Designs and projects: Ho Huu An and Laurence Arnac/www.kirigami.fr
Photography: Jean-Baptiste Pellerin
Styling: Dominique Turbé
Graphic design and layout: Either studio

First published in Great Britain 2013 by Search Press Limited,
Wellwood, North Farm Road, Tunbridge Wells, Kent TN2 3DR

Original edition © 2012
World rights reserved by Éditions Marie Claire
Original French title: *Kirigami: cartes pop-up et motifs à découper*

ISBN: 978-1-84448-994-7

Printed in Malaysia